$9 THERAPY

Semi-Capitalist Solutions

to Your Emotional Problems

$9 THERAPY

Megan Reid & Nick Greene

MORROW GIFT
An Imprint of WILLIAM MORROW

DEDICATED TO THE SANCTUM

&

IN MEMORY OF BEANS

CONT

ENTS

INTRODUCTION

We wanted to write a book that takes self-care seriously without taking *itself* too seriously.

Yes, eventually you will need to take a shower, brush your teeth, and pull yourself together so that you at least RESEMBLE a normal human. But let us mildly misinterpret journalist and bestselling author Dan Harris for a moment: we think that sometimes spending nine dollars or less on an act of self-care will make you a fraction happier. And thank God that usually that fraction is all you need to turn your day around.

$9 Therapy is a collection of our favorite ways to brighten up a day—without worrying your bank account.

We met while working our first, seemingly prestigious, but literally below-minimum-wage jobs out of school. Trust us, we are not eager to relive our days of scrounging for quarters to buy vending-machine instant ramen. But this time did teach us an appreciation of little things (like a friend with five cents to spare, for example), and we emerged from our twenties with a firm belief in the radical power of simple pleasures. We learned the value of mindfully repotting a plant that was sure to wither in two weeks, selecting a (potentially haunted) painting off the curb, or finally drinking from a decent wineglass—even if we could afford only one.

As you can tell, this is not quite a guide to getting your shit together. We're still working on that . . . and also, isn't hegemony kind of super boring? But the hacks and mini-upgrades in this book are about making your life simpler. More stylish. Better organized. Making you feel comfortable in your home. Relaxed in your workplace. A tiny bit more Zen when you're meeting someone for the first time or trying a new thing. You'll find easy recipes and projects to fill a depressing afternoon when you really CANNOT EVEN.

Don't get us wrong: we completely believe in the value of actual, professional therapy. Not all kinds are for everyone, but we know that therapy is more than just self-care. Both of us have found it essential not just for our emotional lives, but for our physical and intellectual ones as well. There are no quick fixes.

But, in a world where everything from weed to journaling to near-starvation diets fall under the self-care heading, we can at least reframe therapeutic choices as something fun that won't break the bank. In this book, we want to share some tricks that make life a little bit easier, a little bit less stressful, a little bit better, a little more loving toward ourselves and the humans around us.

Our tips are a mix of quick pointers and ideas that need a little bit more explaining. To get a sense of the kinds of hacks we get

REALLY excited about, flip to the essays we're calling "Letters of Recommendation." You know how the best thing to mock about self-important lifestyle gurus is their single-minded conviction that they know All the Best Things Ever That They Just Can't Help But Share in Great Enthusiastic Detail? Yup, we're like that too . . . except about consensual no-strings sex and friends who are witches and Joan Didion.

That said, there's no wrong way to use this book, whether you read it all the way through or skip around to the beauty recipes or staycation itineraries that get you off. You were smart enough to pick this up—you're smart enough to figure out how to make this shit work for you.

We know consumerism won't solve all your problems—because, like, late capitalism IS the problem. Packing a perfect suitcase and drinking filtered water won't change your life. But if spending nine bucks helps you get started toward happier living?

That's not a bad deal.

Here's some advice we've gotten from other self-help books:

"Eat Organic." With what trust fund?

"Watch a High School Play." Sounds triggering, tbh.

"Hire a Personal Trainer." We have been scamming ourselves into gym "student discount trials" since the day we graduated.

"Get Biofeedback Analysis." Actually, this is a great reminder to schedule a dentist appointment. . . .

"Lie in the Light of the Full Moon." Does a happy lamp count?

All of this sounds great—really!—but it's just not realistic for us . . . or, like, anyone on a budget that isn't infinite.

So maybe . . .

- ✖ You have a foam roller, but not a subscription to an infrared sauna.
- ✖ You live somewhat cheaply, but also enjoy the good life.
- ✖ You follow Instagram accounts with aspirational aesthetics and have been known to shamelessly swipe a discarded

bookcase from the curb and paint it Scandinavian white. (If not, by the end of the book, you will totally want to.)

✶ You're quite willing to spend money on yourself, but still haven't super-duper started a 401(k).

✶ You want to see yourself with the trappings of adulthood, like kids, careers, degrees . . . or maybe just a dog and West Elm furniture . . . but you recognize that capitalism is literally out to make us feel miserable about ourselves.

✶ You reallllllly don't want to break a twenty on anything other than happy hour.

✶ You only want to make things you'll ACTUALLY use.

✶ You take mental health seriously, but also realize that it's a little weird that we talk to our analysts more often than our parents.

✶ You snark about #selfcare, but realize that, hey—we need it to keep going in a world that devalues our identities.

✶ In short . . . it us. And we bet it's you, too.

CHAPTER 1

ON SCAMMING YOUR COWORKERS

> " Two words: happy lamps. "

COSPLAY FOR THE JOB YOU WANT

It's totally okay to create an office persona. You're a fucking sparkly perfect soul of a human already, of course, but with apologies to every work wife we've ever had, there's something very attractive about keeping a line between your nine-to-five and five-to-nine lives. Besides helping you cultivate an aura of unflappable cool, staying tight-lipped will often endear you to your coworkers more than baring your soul. Literally *no one* at your retail job cares that you drunk texted your neighbor at 3 a.m., so stop talking about it.

And not to be too much of a fake, but drawing a veil over your after-hours hours can also help you try out being the self-actualized person you want to be. Spice up your space like you're the high-flying creative/intellectual/financial/service-oriented CEO you want to be. Pin up a printout of fitness classes from the closest over-priced studio—no one has to know you haven't taken your ass to the gym in six months. Frame a photo of the dog you're totally going

> **Put an air plant in a company mug.**

to get when your tax refund comes in. You'll look so together that maaaybe no one will notice you definitely spilled half a Manhattan on the quizzes you were supposed to be grading.

MAKE A NOT-TO-DO LIST

Management theory holds that organizations are much more successful when they focus on what their missions are. The takeaway for you? The most important part of prioritization is figuring out what you're *not* going to do. That could be as simple as logging out of Facebook so your entire afternoon isn't spent scrolling. Or it could be setting a goal with your manager that you are no longer in charge of unjamming the photocopier. Once you realize what you can do without in the workplace (whether that's shutting down Outlook and Slack every day while you eat your sad desk salad, streamlining check request workflow, or cutting off that coworker who recaps *Married to Medicine* for fifteen minutes at the coffeemaker every morning), you'll get a better sense of what kind of work fulfills you and is worth your time.

> **Decorate your cubicle with wrapping paper sheets.**

"GET YOUR SHIT TOGETHER" DAY

Weekends.* Finally a time to tune out the expectations of your boss, parents, society, humankind, yourself, whomever. Alas, we all know there are one million and one tiny tasks you've put off in the days since last weekend. If you're like us, and you don't have servants, you've got way too much going on to relax on the weekend. Like handwashing that cardigan you wear too often. Or paying that bill you haven't opened since the weekend before last. And did you ever return that fast-fashion dress that fits only mannequins? *This shit weighs you down.* You can't properly enjoy your brunches, yogalates, sliding scale acupuncture, or farmers' marketing when the vibe is dead by the thousand cuts of chores, catching up on mail, and figuring out what to do about that slightly scary situation blooming under your bathroom sink.

---

* Or whichever days of the week or parts of days are your break from work.

> **"** Keep fuzzy socks at your desk. **"**

We don't have a $9 solution to make your bills stop coming (turns out it's very expensive to change your identity or fake your own death). But we can share a simple trick that our friends on the *Call Your Girlfriend* podcast taught us. Choose one day a month when you promise yourself you'll finally open that scary IRS mail or donate that weird dress: a "Get Your Shit Together" Day.

Setting up your Shit Together Day is easy! We do it on our birthdate each month. Find a way to remind yourself, be it a recurring calendar event or a circled day each month in your planner—whatever works for you. And on that day, you just have to pick a couple of the most annoying things on that endless to-do list that you can't even find anymore.

One great Shit Together Day activity is to log on to your bank account (ugh, I know) and go down the list of transactions looking for any recurring bills you don't use or can consolidate (or pay for one of those apps that does it for you). Do you *really* need a sub-

> **Find your perfect pen.**
> **You deserve better than your office**
> **manager's stutter rollerballs.**

scription to Netflix, Hulu, HBO Now, *and* Amazon Prime? No, you don't. (And hot tip: they'll all be one great conglomerate soon, anyway.) Borrow a password from somebody. This isn't the nineties. And we're what? Unbundling.

Do a deep clean, or part of a deep clean. Empty out all your kitchen cabinets and throw out the open baking soda or your former roommate's molding sriracha, the one he left before facing the reality that sustaining a music career was less workable than joining the family insurance business.

What's under your bed? No, really, is it something you're ever going to use again? Toss out that box of musty sweaters and vacuum up the zoo of dust bunnies down there.

Call somebody back.

CHAPTER 2

ADULTING FOR PLEASURE AND PROFIT

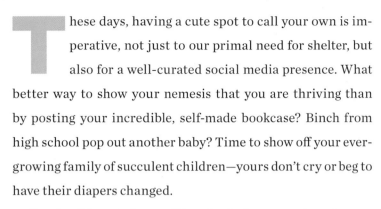

These days, having a cute spot to call your own is imperative, not just to our primal need for shelter, but also for a well-curated social media presence. What better way to show your nemesis that you are thriving than by posting your incredible, self-made bookcase? Binch from high school pop out another baby? Time to show off your ever-growing family of succulent children—yours don't cry or beg to have their diapers changed.

You don't have to be a millionaire to have a spot you love or at least like. Maybe you already have one, but you can't take it to the next level because every time you open Pinterest you're overwhelmed by an avalanche of DIY projects for people with seemingly unlimited time. Never fear! *$9 Therapy* is here. As with day drinking, decorating your apartment is a marathon, not a sprint. With this handful of little projects you know you can actually get done, you'll feel calmer and less stressed than those gut-reno home bloggers ever could.

HIDE YOUR MESS

Life is messy, but your space doesn't have to be. And you don't have to spend your life savings on custom closet cabinetry for

your place to look tidy. (On that note, if you haven't read *The Life-Changing Magic of Tidying Up* by Marie Kondo, drop this book and read that one.) The first step toward organized living is getting rid of all the stuff you never use and don't need. The first time Nick tried it, he got rid of two-thirds of his clothes, three-quarters of his books, and a one very toxic fuckbuddy; Meg has never felt more accomplished than when she unballed her hardworking socks.

Now that you've read (or watched, no judgment) Marie Kondo, it is time to turn your attention to the way you keep stuff. As our friend and illustrator Nathan W. Pyle put it, "Let us store irregular shapes inside shapes with flat surfaces." In other words, boxes are your friends. In your purge, be sure to keep any sturdy shoeboxes for storing your now properly paired socks. That iPhone box you've been holding on to for a year is a perfect pen organizer if you pull out the phone-shaped casket inside. That hairball of mismatched cords in your nightstand? Disentangle them, twist-tie them into little bows, and drop 'em in an empty Ziploc bag. It seems stupid, but after a week of being able to go into a drawer without dreading the four-minute hunt for a clean, matching pair of socks you'll never look back.

If you've got a little budget to spare for *decorganizing*, check out a cord holder for under your desk, media stand, or TV altar. At the end of the day, it's really just a box that encloses a power strip—

> " **You're worth fresh flowers every week.** "

you could use a particularly pleasant shoebox—but you'll feel like fucking Martha Stewart if you're not physically or visually tripping over that ball of cords.

And if you're a real weekday warrior, invest in a phone stand and stop knocking over your coffee trying to prop up your internet rectangle. They can range from a simple scoop that keeps the thing upright to a wireless charger that lets you see and ignore texts without the immense bother of lifting your head or craning your neck.

Also, pouches aren't just for kangaroos anymore. They can be useful for anything from on-the-go charging solutions to makeup to pencils to bigger things like workout shoes. Bags within bags will shave time off your commute, reduce stress when you're at 3 percent battery, and look cool when your friend asks if they can borrow whatever: *Oh, it's in my bag, in the gold lamé pouch.*

Secure the bag!

The most magical thing about living in the modern age is that we can finally control the temperature. Except all of that so-hot-in-winter-your-knuckles-crack and so-cold-in-summer-that-only-dudes-in-suits-are-happy air is out to get your complexion and sinuses.

TRICK #1: Pint-sized humidifier diffusers are all of $5 online. Buy one for your bedroom, your office, your car. Your pores will soak in all of those tiny water molecules and thank you with less oil, less chapping, and dewiness that you can normally get only from over-priced cult makeup brands.

TRICK #2: It is a truth universally acknowledged that drinking water is boring, unless it's poured from a carafe. There is zero fun in filling a basic Ikea glass with tap water; but it's easy to trick yourself that you're at a fancy hotel if you first fill a *fancy container* with water, and *then* pour it into an Ikea glass. Hint: this is also a good way to make your and your roommates' cobbled-together dish sets look like they match.

It's called cognitive behavioral therapy—look it up!

Also, a quick note on the crafts in this book:

Even though we're trying to fix your life, here, we're not those earnest, crafty types you see on Instagram needlepointing "The Future Is Female" into samplers or casually building industrial-chic dining room sets for our friends, Aidan from *Sex and the City* style (the worst, most condescending, mansplaining, "nice guy," awkwardly tall boyfriend of the bunch, and you can quote us on that). Frankly, if you're anything like us, when you're in an anxiety spiral the last thing ANYONE wants in your hands is a knitting needle. But it feels so productive to MAKE things sometimes, you know? Especially if those things take no more than two or three steps and are ready to use that day and will make you feel just slightly superior to your roommate who spent the last two hours listening to podcasts in his boxers. Things you can touch and hold and . . . yes, filter to absolute perfection on Instagram.

Marbled Carafe

WHAT YOU'LL NEED:

A glass, dishwasher-safe container. (Please don't buy a
real carafe. Take pride in how much of a wino/hipster
you are and reuse a fancy rosé bottle or mason jar.)
Nail polish. (Please don't buy specific nail polish for

(continued)

> " Curate two "in case of emergencies" work playlists: one for bops to amp you up, one with chill favorites and soundscapes to calm you down. "

this. This is when you use that half-dried old bottle of Chanel Le Vernis in Black Satin that you bought with half your savings account in 2010 and used once before you realized you aren't eighteen years old.)

Liquid dish soap

A bowl or large Tupperware container

Paper towels

HOW YOU'LL DO IT:

1. Fill the bowl with hot water—not boiling, but as hot as your tap can provide.

2. Depending on the bowl's size, add 2 to 5 drops of liquid soap atop the water. This creates a tension layer for the nail polish, helping it float instead of sinking to the bottom.

3. Slowly pour in the nail polish. Don't add it all in one area—swirl it around, and gently tip the bowl to create marbled patterns until most of the water's surface is covered.

4. Dip the bottom of your container into the water, removing it slowly enough that the polish sticks to the glass. Be sure not to get any of the nail polish too close to the container's rim. While nail polish dries to be dishwasher-safe, it's best not to sip directly from the painted area, in case of chips.

5. Turn your carafe upside down on a drying rack or paper towel to dry.

6. Fill your carafe up with water, lemon, and cucumbers and arrange glasses around it picturesquely. Tag a fancy spa on Instagram and challenge them to get on your level.

> **Curate a desk bar—borrow unopened bottles from the holiday party for a rainy day.**

CREATE A CAREER VISION BOARD—ONE TOO REAL TO KEEP AT WORK

Cut out stuff that represents where you want to be in five years: dreamy office spaces from decor mags, newspaper reviews of inspiring work in your field, or just shit you wanna buy when you're rich.

DO NOT bring this to the office. That'd be embarrassing and potential grounds for firing. Instead, focus on the three biggest themes from your vision-boarding to manifest. Write them on Post-its and put them where you'll see them every day.

DECLUTTER YOUR TECH

There's no reason your home screen needs to be a mess of apps and drafts of files from God knows when. Calm it down and clear it out.

* A streamlined desktop is a beautiful thing . . . even if all you've done is drag files into a folder named DESKTOP.
* Change your settings so screenshots automatically end up in their own folder. Nothing's more embarrassing than going to

show your manager a six-month budget projection and accidentally opening Gchats from your ex or dumb cat memes.

* Delete all gifs from your text messages in settings.
* Color-code your apps.
* Get rid of all your marketing emails because you don't have money anyway. Search for the word "unsubscribe" in your in-box. Then select all and hit Spam.

LETTER OF RECOMMENDATION: $9 WAYS TO MAKE A DIFFERENCE

* Phone bank
* Register voters
* Work the polls on election day. (You get paid for it!)
* Go to town hall meetings.
* Call out racists, transphobes, and misogynists—especially if you're male, cis, het, or benefit from white privilege.
* Lend support and offer your talents to people you know. Can you let your friends who are working parents know that you're on call for last-minute babysitting shifts? Can you tutor the kid next door for an hour a week? Can you

get your office to participate in a recycling program? Can you design a flyer for food banks/yoga studios/library book drives?

These next tips are especially good for the socially anxious (aka, US) who immediately begin panicking at the thought of participating in a demonstration or march.

* Read the news. Get straight on your values. Figure out what issues matter to you and form an opinion on your own before joining a conversation.
* If you can afford it, don't spend money at companies that engage in practices that are against your ethics.
* Putting $9 where your mouth is can make a giant impact. Set up a monthly auto-pay on your debit or credit card for your favorite charity, activist, or artist.
* Foster animals. Usually, you get the food and supplies for free while waiting for the pet to get a great home.

> **"**
> Paint of all your furniture Scandinavian white.
> **"**

> "New sheets are expensive. But high thread-count pillowcases? Those you can afford."

✶ Expand your comfort zone. Realize that the world is bigger than your experience.

WHITE VINEGAR

Fact: This shit fixes everything. Streaks on your mirrors, grout in your shower, grime on your floor. Boil some with water when your kitchen smells frounzy. Pour a cup of it with half a cup of baking soda down your drains every two weeks. Add half a cup to your laundry when you wash your sweaty gym clothes. Run 1 cup vinegar with 1 cup water through your coffee machine twice a month or so—unless you like drinking mildew. White vinegar is cheap enough to buy by the gallon, and it's just as useful in a basic salad dressing or marinade as a fancy flavored balsamic.

Those scary, passive-aggressive real estate couples make it look easy on your mom's HGTV shows, but certain home hacks DO require professional attention. An inexhaustive list of when to definitely NOT fix things around the house:

* When it involves electricity.
* When it involves heights higher than a stepladder.
* When you're drunk or high.
* When you could just buy the damn thing more cheaply.
* When it's less than two weeks after a breakup.
* When there's literally no replacing it.
* When it's fixing something that costs more than your monthly paycheck.
* When you're missing a key accessory (for example, hanging shelves without a leveler, trying to use a butter knife as a screwdriver, etc.).
* When your landlord will kick you out if you fuck it up.

GOOD SMELLS MATTER

We're sure you shower daily and change your sheets at least (*at least!*) every three weeks. Good on you!

But even if you always air out the kitchen after you fry up bacon for hangover brunch, take out the trash as soon as it's full, and never, ever let your dog sit on the couch after it's tracked in God-knows-what from the sidewalk, you're only human. And smelling like a human is a human part of being … well … human. In addition to the basic hygiene you're practicing, you can level up with these two cheap hacks.

DIY LINEN AND ROOM SPRAY

There's nothing better than sliding into freshly scented sheets. They're indulgent, relaxing, and transporting, and everyone will want to crawl between them, which is helpful for convincing humans to sleep with you. It's also surprisingly inexpensive to dupe store-bought versions and customize a blend that speaks to you.

1. Buy a spray bottle from the dollar store.
2. Fill it one-third of the way with vodka, and then fill it to the top with water.
3. Depending on the size of the spray bottle and your scent preferences, add 10 to 20 drops of essential oil. Feel free to combine scents: orange and clove, lavender and lemon, and ylang-ylang and geranium are all winners.
4. Spray the concoction on your bedsheets, upholstered furniture, rugs, or anywhere that needs a refresh. Feel free to make extras for the bathroom or to passive-aggressively gift to your gross roommate.

CANDLES!

As the great John Waters once said, "If you go home with some-body, and they don't have candles, don't fuck 'em!" Or something like that. The patriarchy makes us reward men for all sorts of dumb shit, and we can think of at least two otherwise unim-pressive young men who tipped the hookup scales in their favor

PURELY by having candles and a couple of living houseplants. If basic dudes who suck at returning texts can do it, so can you.

The cost of materials upfront means that it's not worth it to make these, in our opinion (unless it's for fun), so feel free to buy. But although those people at Diptyque know what they're doing by somehow convincing you to literally burn your hard-earned money into nothingness, it is honestly just as effective to grab a bagful of scented tea lights or pillars next time you're at the grocery store. Rather than risk an allergy attack with something called Oceanside Cinnamon-Cucumber, keep it simple with a basic woody or floral scent.

OPT OUT OF JUNK MAIL

Yes, really, it is possible to cease the merciless onslaught of crap you get in the mail—without throwing out that health insurance reimbursement that your landlord needs. *(Props to junk mail influencer Whitson Gordon of the* New York Times *for the tips.)*

STEP 1: CREDIT CARDS, LOANS, AND INSURANCE. Go to the Federal Trade Commission website and search "unsolicited mail." That takes you to a website where you fill in your stats (including social security number), which

will alert the credit bureaus not to let unwanted financial advice find you.

STEP 2: ALL THE OTHER JUNK IN YOUR TRUNK. To free yourself of the tyranny of unwanted catalogs, go to dmachoice.thedma.org/register.php. Looks shady AF and asks you to pony up two dollars, but in our experience, the joy of coming home to an empty mailbox several times a week is worth the fee.

GLUE GUN, FIX MY LIFE

The VIP of DIY accoutrements is, by a long shot, the humble glue gun. One of these babies will cost you less than a tenner at your local craft supply store and can be used solo for all sorts of common home hacks.

SLIPPERY RUGS. So, you don't want to buy backing for that bathmat you got on sale at Restoration Hardware and are shamelessly using as office decor, but you keep almost falling on your ass whenever you move to pull out your desk chair? The sticky yet pliable glue from one of these will keep rag rugs stable. Just draw triangles on each corner of the underside and let them dry. It works better to keep rugs in place than those weird foam liners.

QUICK NO-SEW CURTAINS. Curtains, shower curtains, wall hangings: oh, the things you can do with a cute piece of fabric and a glue gun! Make your windows look more polished than hanging sheets over them with tacks by taking your favorite wall hanging by the shortest side. Measure five inches down from the top, then fold the fabric down to create a loop. Tuck the raw side in for polish, then glue the folded loop horizontally. Thread your curtain rod through the loop and congratulate yourself.

BEER/MUG KOOZIES. Your tall wool socks with holes in the toes are embarrassing, and your hands are too warm/too cold around your beverages. Kill two birds with one stone.

Your thickest socks are best for this one. Turn the offending sock inside out and cut just above where the "heel" of the sock angles into the sock's shaft. Lay the remaining fabric flat in a rectangle, and drizzle the glue randomly so that most of the fabric is covered. Scrunch artistically, but let some of the glue remain exposed as it dries: This will keep the Koozie in place. Repeat on the other side of the rectangle. Turn it right side out and go buy yourself a six-pack. You've earned it.

MAKEUP BRUSH CLEANER. "DIY makeup brush cleaner" may be the most on-brand thing we've ever googled, so get ready for us to drop some brilliant/stupid-simple knowledge. Take literally any nonflammable surface you don't care that much about (your last remaining coaster, an old CD) and make patterns on it with the glue gun. They can really be any shape, but the heights and thickness of the glue should vary. Let it dry, and you have a makeup brush cleaning mat. All the influencers have one; it's a thing you didn't know you wanted, but you really do need.

And please use it. We can 99 percent guarantee that if you're a normal human with a job and friendships and responsibilities, you haven't even thought about your makeup brushes in months, because life is short and fleeting, etc. But honestly. Your brushes are disgusting. Do your pores a favor.

NONSLIP (NONDAMAGING) HANGERS. Silky, lacy, strappy tops and dresses deserve better than constantly sliding off your Ikea hangers into a pile on your closet floor. Squeeze a thin line of hot glue on the top of your hangers' angled edges and allow it to cool before hanging your clothes. Once it dries, your stuff isn't moving an inch, no matter how delicate your one nice blouse is.

"RUSTIC" "BOOKSHELVES"

We know these work, and here's how:

One of our best friends, Tyler, made the delightful decision to marry a French man. Like, really French. As in, marinière-wearing, family-has-a-vineyard, chain-smoking, bread-snob, nonironic Serge Gainsbourg–listening, dark-haired, blue-eyed, judgy-AF Frenchman. His name is Martin, but you have to say it Mahr-tan, and he makes us *gougères*.

So, since he is perfect in literally every way, of course he turned us on to this hack.

Wine. Cases. Are. Perfect. Bookshelves.

Not only are the wooden versions generally proper cuts of wood rather than PVC, they're sturdy enough to hold twelve bottles: more than adequate for your paperbacks. The blond wood cases that are most companies' go-to are very Danish chic, and the stamps on the exteriors only serve to prove that you've matured beyond $3 PBR orders.

Your local wine store should be happy to hook you up for free, if you go on recycling day. Turn one sideways to have it double as end table storage; stack two or more for bookcase realness.

LETTER OF RECOMMENDATION: THE MEDITATION NOOK

There are so many things to be properly, righteously, furiously angry about in this world. Gun violence is a more likely form of death than suffocating, drowning, or thyroid cancer. Twenty percent of Americans think interracial marriage is "morally wrong." There's an entire CONTINENT of trash floating in the northern Pacific Ocean. Ten million kids around the world are trafficked and forced into labor.

And, not to be flip, those "big issues" don't even encompass the little slights and heartbreaks of being human every day. Manspreaders. Overdraft fees on your debit card. Spilling your coffee on the presentation you stayed up all night to finish. Unrequited love, for the fiftieth time. A lifetime's worth of microaggressions. Chronic pain. A broken fingernail, or tooth, or pinky toe.

Sadly, "calm" and "happy" aren't really things you can make tangible. But you CAN control at least a tiny slice of your physical space, and set up a zone specifically for those two things to flourish—or, at least, to escape from the rest of the trappings of a shitty day.

Enter the meditation nook.

In the most basic sense, all you need for a meditation nook is a spot where you can sit comfortably. Even if you share a room or have a billion roommates or your apartment looks over a subway track, you can create a place where the only purpose is to tune in to yourself. It can be more symbolic if you're truly cramped: maybe your "nook" is a blanket you fold at the foot of your bed or a chair off to the side on the roof of your apartment complex or a spot on your living room floor facing a blank corner.

If a meditation nook sounds too woo-woo for you (NEVER MIND that mindfulness is a central precept of basically every school of philosophy and religious framework from antiquity to the present day), keep in mind that there's logic in connecting intention to space. Setting aside a physical place in your house where you do nothing but chill the fuck out will make that idea more concrete.

Also, feel free to call this a "chill the fuck out" nook if you like; language is ever-morphing and symbolic anyway.

For traditional mindfulness, a seat and your breath are all you need. You don't have to add any spiritual energy to it: look at all the finance bros who meditate so they can "go hard" and "power up." But seeing as this book is written by two Capricorns who definitely know what's best for you, we WILL say that adding items to supplement your nook's good vibes is a great idea! Feel free to incorporate anything that represents how you want to feel when you're most relaxed: aware, safe, grounded, peaceful, what- have-you. Lighting some palo santo or smudging a little sage above your nest of tranquility is a highly suggested tip, but be creative and play with your instincts.

Some ideas in increasing order of hippie-dippieness:

* A cushion (you might hear people call the special round ones for meditation zafus, but anything that helps you sit with your knees lower than your hips is cool)
* An eye mask
* A blanket to cover yourself while you sit
* A comfy rug

- Plants
- Tea lights
- Incense or essential oils
- Himalayan salt lamps
- Photos of loved ones or special places
- Symbols of your spiritual traditions: mandalas, figures of Ganesha or the Buddha, crucifixes, mala beads, images of ancestors, etc.
- Crystals
- Herbs, shells, and feathers
- Tarot cards

LETTER OF RECOMMENDATION: SEX IS FUN

One free way you can entertain yourself is to have sex with another human being. Sex has numerous documented health benefits, like endorphins and some coronary stuff we don't fully remember and refuse to google at work. It's a thing everyone should do. And, truly, you don't even really need another human being to do it well.

But if you choose to do it with one (or more!) other humans, here's what you'll do:

1. Find a human you're reasonably attracted to.
2. Verify they will not hurt you emotionally or physically in nonconsensual ways.
3. Lure them to your bedroom with some flimsy pretense about Netflix or installing shelving.
4. Remove your clothes and try to not be anxious.

If you're lucky, you can pass a couple hours this way and then fall asleep before having to learn the names of their siblings!

LETTER OF RECOMMENDATION: ENCHANT YO'SELF

So a couple of years ago (around, say . . . November of 2016, *ahem*), basically every bitch in Brooklyn became a witch?

Faster than you could say *The Craft*, our friends began following crystal suppliers on Instagram and reading tarot and knowing the difference between the new and full moon. Lots of people had been doing this stuff for actual millennia, to be fair. But suddenly, the idea of witchcraft was being weaponized against cultural norms like heterosexism, patriarchy, and misogyny. "What is empowering about witchcraft is that it models and references access to a power that is not conditional, something that cannot be bestowed or taken away by others or by circumstance, but that is intrinsic to your being because you're a living creature on earth," says Mya Spalter, author of *Enchantments: A Modern Witch's Guide to Self-Possession.* "I think different mysticisms and forms of magic—witchcrafts—are methods of studying how we can make the best use of what we already have." Practical, affirming, compassionate, and the perfect toolkit for the forthcoming revolution.

"With this comes a whole new buffet of rituals, most of which have been handed down from generation to generation," says Crystal Fawn, one of our favorite magical humans, and a light worker who consults her clients on using psychic insight in everyday life.

Look, the word "witch" brings up a LOT for some people. Meg, for instance, was raised in an evangelical, first-generation Caribbean American home, so yeah—even reading Harry Potter was an early indicator that she was going to become very in touch with her birth chart. We get that some people aren't comfortable with *brujería* in any form and that science exists and we definitely, definitely think that vaccinating your kids and getting a fucking flu shot is a better idea that chanting some spell an "influencer" wrote for you. What we're pushing toward here is getting better at practicing habits that feel personal to you, and tapping into the what you know you know— those gut feelings, flashes of insight, and intuitive moments that more often than not get ignored when time is tight and shit is stressful.

Oh, and there are ways to bring more magic into your life without being an asshole to, you know, ACTUAL witches. Though per Crystal, "we're finally seeing traditional religion fall a little by the wayside, with more and more of the population identifying as 'spiritual,' instead of 'practicing,'" maybe don't appropriate other cultural heritages? "There are witches who think of their practice as religion or a set of philosophical principles and practices that they have been entrusted with. For instance, calling yourself a witch or *bruja* or *santera* or high priestess might be an important signifier and distinction within your community, a title that you've earned through lineage, experience, and study," Mya says.

That caveat in mind: Go the fuck ahead and claim your magic. Maybe for you, magic is remembering that the ginger tea your grandma always forced you to drink when you had a sore throat actually made you feel better than NyQuil ever has. Maybe it's being more aware of the fact that you're the only one of your friends whose plants are still alive and recognizing that as a gift, not coincidence. Maybe it's paying a little more attention to your intuition when deciding whether or not to bring home some random from the bar (this requires not being 100 percent shitfaced, so low-key work on that, too). And Mya agrees that we aren't just being trite, here. "I think it's impossible not to incorporate aspects of magic into your life! You don't need to be a chef to cook food. Everyone can apply heat to something raw, and they've technically done some cooking, right? I think it's the same with magic. . . . We're all applying our will to things, we all have some idea of how to mirror our internal world in the external world through our choices of sights, sounds, smells, tastes and textures to bring about a certain vibe or effect (if I say dim light, saxy music, roses, chocolate, satin, you have an idea of the feeling I'm projecting/altar I'm building)."

With that in mind, enjoy the following from Crystal, a *$9 Therapy* spell just for you:

My particular brand of spiritualism focuses on energy—which is neither good nor bad, it just IS—and ways in which it's shared across time and space. All dimensions welcome!

Keep in mind that not everyone is practicing the same magic, and inquire about a practitioner's ethics before following any advice. Personally, I believe that the highest goal for all of us is to be of service. That what you're experiencing on an individual level is important, but that you need to spend as much energy as you can spare helping those who need it. The trick is figuring out a happy balance so that your energy is protected but also made available to others. It's hard, but totally worth it!

Okay, so this energy . . . a lot of times I'll hear of instances in which someone is being jerked around by another person. This can be a landlord, a lover, a family member, etc. The best remedy I've found for this is called a Freezing Spell. My mom taught it to me when I was maybe nine or ten years old and it's never failed me.

To counteract someone stealing your mojo (and sanity), write the following on a piece of paper:

<Full Name> has no power over me, <Your Full Name>

Mentally
Physically
Financially
Emotionally
Spiritually

Thank you, <God, Universe, Powers That Be, etc.>!

Now place the paper in a spare Tupperware container and fill it with water. Keep the paper submerged! In fact, layer a few ice cubes on it to hold it down. Put the whole shebang in your freezer. Netflix and chill.

Depending on your time frame, or the power of the human in question, try to thaw and dry out the paper on a full moon. Sometimes this is a few weeks later. Sometimes it's a few years. Totally your call. Once it feels like the right time, burn it—the paper, not the Tupperware—in a safe place.

Disclaimer: This spell doesn't "do" anything to the other person. If you imagine that long tunnel of energy from *Donnie Darko* (or even *Stargate*) that's pretty much what people are doing to each other on a regular basis. Sometimes people are needy or controlling with their vortex, which means no matter how many sticks of incense you burn there is an overwhelming sense of frustration or ickiness. What this spell does is "freeze" that energy tunnel, giving you some freedom to basically stop obsessing about whatever it is this person has terrorized you with. Safe to use on friends and family!

CHAPTER 3

ENTERTAIN LIKE AN INFLUENCER

We like to party. But our least favorite party game is debit card roulette: *Will or won't the bank decline my card after I generously but foolishly agreed to foot the entire bar tab?* If, like us, you want to be socially fabulous on a budget, just have everybody over to your place. That way, you can split the cost of wine and food, and get to show off all the hard work you've put into painting your entire home Scandinavian white (see page 27).

Other perks of playing host:

* Leftover wine.
* Control of the playlist.
* No embarrassing themes.
* No enemies.
* Your favorite Gatorade the morning after (see page 78).
* Ability to kick out randoms at will.
* Social cachet leading to world domination.

We've put together an infallible combo of tricks, tips, and recipes to make you seem like the hostess with the mostest, even if you're really the hostess with the stingiest budget.

ICE CUBE TRAYS

Funny-shaped ice cube trays can either make you *très chic* (spheres, cubes) or make you laugh (penguins, genitalia). Mix in herbs or booze—hell, make wine Popsicles.

STEAL YOUR GRANDMA'S GLASSES

You know those bizarre, smoky glasses with, like, silvered rims that your grandmother had in the basement somewhere? They looked absurd with her gingham tablecloths. But in your newly Scandinavian white, Pinterest trap apartment (no, we will NOT stop suggesting this), they will look more like *objets*. The Salvation Army is always overflowing with them.

UNEXPECTED CENTERPIECE

A tablescape is an artful pile of objects that enhances a meal's aesthetic and sparks conversation. Throw candles on any of these and—voilà! *Architectural Digest.*

- ✱ Attractive books you want to show off.

- ✱ Hand-drawn pics of your guests (even if they're really bad).

- ✱ Pretty branches and leaves (check for bugs).

- ✱ Mugs with tea lights floating in them.

- ✱ Kids' toys: Rubik's Cubes, Play-Doh, fidget spinners, brain puzzles. Give the awkward ones something to do.

EAT AND DRINK

Cooking for yourself and friends could be stressful, but we're not about that Julia Child life. The recipes we're sharing are some of the most party-ready ones we know. You should be able to focus on your friends while making them. They're meant to be improvisational—as long as you follow the spirit of the dish you should end up with something totally edible. So please replace ingredients you don't like with ones you do. And don't panic if you've kept a pot on the stove for five extra minutes, or you put in one pinch of salt where we suggested two. Put on a playlist, break out the vape, and roll with it. We promise you won't fuck this up.

Positivity Pasta Sauce

You're basically Ina Garten now.

WHAT YOU'LL NEED

One 28-ounce can of crushed tomatoes (spend that
   extra dollar for the fancy kind)
Two pinches oregano (dried is fine)
Salt and pepper to taste
Butter or butter substitute
Fresh (paycheck permitting) basil

HOW YOU'LL DO IT

1. Empty the tomatoes and their juice into a bowl. Mush 'em up with the oregano, salt, and pepper.
2. Pour it all into a saucepan over medium-low heat.
3. Add 1 to 2 tablespoons of butter to the pan and let it melt with a sprig of basil for 15 to 20 minutes (or until it sticks to the back of a spoon).
4. Pour over any kind of pasta you like. Garnish with another sprig of basil.

How easy was that?

Deviled Eggs

Not just for aunties anymore, deviled eggs are making a delicious comeback—and you can almost certainly make them with food you've already got at home.

WHAT YOU'LL NEED

A dozen eggs

¼ cup mayo

1 tablespoon Dijon mustard

1 teaspoon sugar

A plastic ziplock bag, at least 1 gallon

Chopped fresh chives, for garnish (spend money on these; they look fancy)

HOW YOU'LL DO IT

1. Put the eggs in a large pot and fill it with enough water to cover them.
2. Bring to a boil, then reduce the heat and simmer for 10 minutes.
3. Carefully scoop the eggs into a colander with a slotted spoon and run them under cold water.
4. Peel each egg and then cut them in half.

5. Scoop out the yolks into a bowl and beat together with the mayo, mustard, and sugar.

6. Fill the plastic ziplock bag with the yolk mixture, then snip off a corner of the bag, about ¼ inch from the corner.

7. Fill each scooped-out egg half with the mixture by gently squeezing it out of the plastic bag through the hole.

8. Arrange the eggs on a pretty plate or tray and sprinkle with the chopped chives.

Cure-All Chicken Soup

Meg's mom (Michelle Harris, *Grace and Frankie* lover, and all-around babe) found this brilliant recipe for Cambodian chicken soup and modified it into Southeast Asian fusion magic. Make this on a Sunday and freeze leftovers for the next time you have a cold.

Ingredients like ginger and shallots sound fancy, but most grocery stores sell them loose. Buy just as much as you need: one head of garlic, for example, should run you something like fifty cents.

WHAT YOU'LL NEED

4 cups water

4 cups chicken broth (get a big can at the grocery)

Zest and juice of one lime

6 garlic cloves, peeled and smashed (use the side of a
knife or a pot)

Three inches of ginger root, smashed

1 jalapeño pepper

A rotisserie chicken, with meat shredded into bite-size
pieces (freeze the bones, flabby bits, cartilage, etc., to
make broth with—see page 66)

A bunch of scallions, chopped

Basil, parsley, or cilantro (or all three!), for garnish. Fresh
or dry doesn't really matter, this is all to your taste.

1 teaspoon salt

½ teaspoon pepper

Whatever noodles you have on hand (the original recipe
calls for Asian-style rice noodles, but a couple of
handfuls of leftover penne will be just as filling)

HOW YOU'LL DO IT

1. Combine the water, broth, zest, garlic, ginger, jalapeño, a teaspoon of salt and half a teaspoon of pepper and bring it to a boil on high heat. Lower the flame to medium-low and let this simmer for 20 minutes.

2. When you're ready to serve, stir the lime juice, chicken, chopped scallions, and herbs into your broth. The trick is to pour the acidic-spicy-salty goodness over what would normally be a plain old bowl of cooked noodles: when you don't boil them in the soup itself, they stay toothsome, not soggy. Store any remaining broth in a big Tupperware if you want to use it in the next four days. Otherwise, portion it off into individual containers and freeze them for quick meal prep.

(PS: Bring this to your significant other when they're sick; you will look SO good and have such good partner karma forever and ever.)

Broth So Easy You Can Do It in Your Sleep

If you thought making your own bone broth was the preserve of the Martha Stewarts of the world, we're here to blow your mind. Turns out all you have to do is simmer chicken leftovers, herbs, spices, and salt in water for a couple of hours. Really—it's that simple, and you can mix and match whatever ingredients you've got lying around.

HOW YOU'LL DO IT

1. Acquire a chicken carcass—either as a result of roasting a chicken yourself or buying a rotisserie one—and pull off all the good meat and store (or eat, tbh).
2. Chop into big pieces any garlic, carrots, or parsnips you may have lying around.
3. A bay leaf and a tablespoon of whole peppercorns are highly recommended. And if you've got other herbs like thyme and oregano, throw a sprig or two of those in, too.
4. Put the chicken, herbs, and veg into your largest pot and fill it up with water.
5. Bring the pot to a boil, then turn it down to a simmer.

6. Now at this point, you have to wait a couple hours. Although you could do this step in your sleep, we're not going to *recommend* that you leave your stove on and unattended. But you could watch a movie without missing a thing going on in that pot. What you will need to do is periodically sample your brew and add salt to taste. We like it salty, but follow your bliss.

7. You'll know the broth is ready when it tastes like something you'd drink out of a mug.

8. Strain it through a sieve or at least a colander.

9. Drink it straight or use it in place of water for rice or noodles! Or add back that leftover meat for a homemade chicken soup.

Banana Pancakes

WHAT YOU'LL NEED

1 banana

1 egg

Optional: ½ teaspoon baking powder, ½ teaspoon vanilla

HOW YOU'LL DO IT

Smash the banana in a bowl. Slightly overripe ones are great for this. Then add your egg, stirring it all together until it's goopy. If you have baking powder to make them fluffier or you want to flavor them up, add your optional ingredients now. Pour half at a time into a nonstick pan over medium heat, flipping after about 1½ to 2 minutes. Top with peanut butter or maple syrup for the world's quickest gluten-free breakfast to split with your roommates as you share walk of shame stories.

Fancy Popcorn

Looks super chic served in colorful bowls, equally befitting a Super Bowl party as a dinner party.

The only tool you need is a pot you can easily cover. Pour in about ½ cup yellow popcorn kernels with 3 tablespoons olive oil. Cover the pan, and then shake it on the heat until you're all popped up. You know what a bag of the microwave stuff sounds like when it's about to burn—wait for that. Then cut the heat and quickly add one of the following fail-proof flavor mixtures while you still have the popcorn in the hot pan:

Bacon bits + salt + dry thyme

Melted butter + salt + pepper

Curry powder + lemon zest

Grated parmesan cheese (or nutritional yeast if you're vegan) + dried basil

Cinnamon + sugar, with just a pinch of salt

Melted chocolate chips + mini marshmallows

Soy sauce + orange zest

Stir! Serve! Repeat as needed until you're snacked out.

One-Pan Hearty Rice

Easy vegetarian entree or brilliant lazy side dish? YOU DECIDE. Super easy to carry to a potluck.

3 tablespoons of your favorite cooking oil

1 shallot, chopped

Half an onion, chopped

1½ cups rice (we like basmati)

1¼ cups vegetable or chicken stock

¼ cup tomato sauce

1 can chickpeas, drained

Salt to taste (start with a teaspoon and go
  from there)

Black pepper or chili flakes to taste

Extras, depending on bougie-ness, taste, and budget:

A few handfuls of spinach—about ¼ to ½ cup if you're
  using frozen

½ cup mushrooms, quartered

¼ cup slivered almonds

1 carrot, chopped

1 celery stalk, chopped

1 cup chopped brussels sprouts

1 cup diced sweet potato

Chopped parsley (optional)

HOW YOU'LL DO IT

1. Preheat the oven to 400° F.

2. In a large oven-safe skillet (stainless steel or one of those hearty ceramic Dutch ovens), heat the oil over medium heat, adding the shallots and onions and cooking until they're soft (about five minutes). Add the uncooked rice and stir it around so that the oil and aromatics get all up in there.

3. Pour in the stock, pasta sauce, chickpeas, salt, pepper, and add whatever combo of the extras listed earlier that you like and stir.

4. Remove the pan from heat and cover it with aluminum foil with one or two holes poked in it with the tines of a fork. Bake for 15 to 20 minutes, stirring once after five minutes. Have a glass of wine while you wait! Listen to an improvement podcast!

5. When time's up, take a quick taste to be sure it's tender,

and season with salt and pepper to taste. Fluff it up so it looks pretty (some chopped parsley always looks good, if you can afford the flat-leafed Italian kind) and serve. It should feed four people as an entree if you add enough veg, or six as a side dish.

Thai-Style Chicken Salad

WHAT YOU'LL NEED

¼ cup soy sauce

3 teaspoons vinegar

Juice of two limes or one lemon

1 teaspoon red pepper flakes

1 teaspoon sugar

2 tablespoons water

1 garlic clove, diced, or about three shakes of garlic powder

(If by any chance you have it, 1 tablespoon fish sauce would be a GREAT, if slightly-more-than-nine-dollar, addition)

3 boneless, skinless chicken thighs (they're cheaper AND they taste better), diced into 1-inch-square

pieces; OR one drained package of extra-firm tofu, cut into 1-inch-square pieces; OR 3 steak medallions, about 4 ounces each, diced into 1-inch-square pieces

HOW YOU'LL DO IT

1. Stir together all the ingredients except your protein in a large bowl until you have a nice-looking marinade.
2. Add your protein.
3. Cover the bowl with plastic wrap and marinate the chicken or steak for at least half an hour, and up to a day in the fridge; tofu will only need about 10 minutes and a quick toss.
4. While it all marinates, make yourself a salad. We're not gonna walk you through this, we trust you. But carrots, cucumbers, and bean sprouts all pair well with the flavors in this dish.
5. Your dressing just has four ingredients. Mix them together until it tastes good to you. It's the wonder of eating at home!

FOR THE DRESSING

Soy sauce

Peanut butter

(continued)

Sugar

Lime or lemon juice

Then heat a nonstick pan with a tablespoon of vegetable oil over medium-high heat. After three minutes, place your protein in the pan, making sure the pieces don't overlap too much. Ladle in two tablespoons of the marinade, then discard the rest.

HOW YOU'LL SAUTÉ

- Chicken until browned, turning every 30 seconds or so.
- Steak to your desired level of doneness (we recommend medium, so the outside will JUST have turned nice and brown).
- Tofu until heated through, stirring often for about six minutes.

Remove from the heat and let the meat rest for a minute or so. Then scoop atop your salad: you should be able to serve at least two very hungry people, and this is a great one for take-to-work lunches.

Top with cilantro or basil if you've got it!

CHEAP FISHES

Here are some types of fish to know:

Tilapia

Cod

Haddock

Pollock

They're all similar in texture (lean, flaky), taste (light, not too oily), and price (quite inexpensive, even if you're buying sustainable, wild-caught versions). They're the easiest fucking thing to cook in the world, and if you learn nothing else from this book, it should be that you can cook fish and a vegetable for dinner in 15 minutes for WELL under $9.

Buy a fillet or two of the above, based on your hunger level. If the fish costs more than $6.99 per pound in 2052 or whenever you're reading this, I'm sorry our generation didn't fix global warming, but you're probably underwater anyway.

As soon as you get home, heat your oven to 375° F. Drizzle in a tablespoon of extra virgin olive oil in an ovenproof pan. Rinse your fish in cold water, pat it dry, and put it in the pan.

Now, think a little: What kinds of food do you like? Plain

and simple? Rub the fillets with salt, pepper, and a dash more olive oil. Squeeze a lemon over the fish and slide a few slivers of onion underneath. (At the very least, this is an easy go-to with a quick bagged salad.) Want a veggie-heavy meal? Consider vegetables that have a similar cooking time to fish: broccoli, cauliflower, string beans, beet slices, baby carrots, zucchini. They all work, so scatter whatever odds and ends you have lurking in your fridge around the pan among the fillets for an all-in-one type of situation. Or maybe you're yearning for your mom's jerk recipe or your grandmother's shrimp boils. Slather some premade sauce or a spice mix on there!

Just MAKE IT TASTE GOOD TO YOU.

Then, pop it in the oven for 12 minutes. Take it out. Eat. (If you need a side, boiled potatoes are nice and cost about 80 cents a piece. Rice is quick, and there's always the option of a big hunk of bread to sop up any saucy goodness).

French 75

A signature drink is key to your #brand. Upgrade that crappy gin from your roommate's party into a grown-up cocktail with just a little sparkling wine and a twist of lemon.

WHAT YOU'LL NEED

Bubbly wine like prosecco or cava—or champagne,
  if you're a millionaire
That handle of off-brand gin that's been in your cabinet
  since New Year's
A lemon peel
Sugar cubes

HOW YOU'LL DO IT

1. Pilfer some sugar cubes from work. If you're really ambitious you could make simple syrup but, like, in this economy?
2. The ratio of bubbles to gin is 2:1. So if you're making only one drink (lol), put two parts bubbles to one part gin and a sugar cube in a big glass and stir it around with some ice.
3. Straining out the ice, pour that out into your grand-ma's fancy glassware.
4. Garnish with the lemon peel.

You did it!

LETTER OF RECOMMENDATION: HOW TO BE HUNGOVER

All good things must end, including your buzz. And unfortunately, drinking begets more drinking. That pic you shouldn't have posted and that umpteenth glass you shouldn't have poured were both the result of alcohol's chemical effect on your decision-making abilities. So don't sweat it! You made your choices and you had a good time and everybody probably forgot that embarrassing thing you said anyway.

The question is, how do you comport yourself now that you've been so rudely overserved? And the answer is: like a princess.

STEP 1: THE WATER

Water needs to be two places when you're hungover: going down your throat and around your body. So drink up. Being hungover can sap your will to live, much less bathe. But trust us. This is but one small step for hangoverkind that will put you on the road to feeling human again. If you have a tub, soak in something delightfully smelly. Wash your face with a gentle cleanser while you count to 60 (for extra points see "Touch Yourself," page 86). Rise all the oil, makeup, and tequila down the drain.

STEP 2: THE OUTFIT

Just because you're in a self-induced zombie state doesn't mean you have to look like the undead. Pick something comfy and glamorous—as flowy as you can get away with, ideally scarves. Sunglasses and Advil, as the bard sang. Treat it like a game: You're in disguise as a hydrated, functional human being. Have fun with it.

STEP 3: THE COFFEE

It is *mandatory* that you have an iced coffee at this juncture—no other potion has the ability to revive your spirits as an extra-large, caffeinated, clinking, cold, coffee bean nectar of the gawds. Its quality is unimportant, because after all that whiskey, your taste buds are on strike and you won't really be able to taste the difference between Blue Bottle and Dunkin' anyway. The outside temperature is also unimportant. What you need is caffeine in your brain and what you *don't* need is to worry about burning your tongue.

STEP 4: THE PLAN

You have to do *something,* or you'll just wallow in self-loathing. Text someone you *should* be texting. Pick an activity that is fairly low-energy, or at least befits your compromised condition. A movie is great. Museums can work. A stroll in a botanical garden. Light shopping. Don't be a martyr.

STEP 5: THE MEAL

Sometimes, when hungover, we are ravenous. Sometimes we can barely hold down anything. Know your body and know your appetite. But don't forget to eat. You spent the night poisoning yourself. Why not be a dear and get a fruit and veggie smoothie? Go ahead and get the extra agave. Bonus points for added ginger.

STEP 6: THE DOG

You will be tempted to say things like "I am never drinking again." Resist that urge. The hair of the dog is your only way forward. Look, you're already at Step 6; you've been so virtuous up till now. Have a small glass of prosecco or beer. It won't kill you and you'll feel leagues better. Probably.

STEP 7: THE NAP

Let's be honest: Depending on the severity of your condition, this might be the only step you make it through successfully. And you know what? That's fine! We love you, your friends love you, and tomorrow this will all be a silly memory that even you will be in the mood to laugh at.

CHAPTER 4

BEAUTY FOR NONEXPERTS

> **Buy decent tweezers.**

FAKE IT TILL YOU SWEAT IT

A certain trendy gym-that-will not-be-named is famed for sinus-opening cold eucalyptus-scented towels. We wish we could afford memberships. But in the meantime, put a cotton washcloth in a bowl of water with two drops of essential oil for twenty seconds. Pull it out with a pair of tongs (or two forks) and apply to your sweaty, clogged forehead. YouTube a mindfulness video and breathe deeply.

EVEN IF IT'S ALL YOU DO TODAY:

* Floss
* Put on sunscreen
* Drink water
* Sleep

> ## " Take an unbothered selfie. "

PUT VITAMINS ON
YOUR BODY

Eating your vitamins is good, but slathering them on your dehydrated corpse is next level.

- **VITAMINS A AND D OINTMENT**–Pros: Costs an actual dollar; great for lips, knees, elbows, feet, and cuticles; easy to mix into body lotion for an amped-up version of your fave moisturizer; high vitamin content overrides some of the drying potential of petroleum jelly; unscented. Cons: Can take a while to absorb; TECHNICALLY for diaper rash, so rarely has cute packaging.
- **VITAMIN C**–Pros: Powerful antioxidant; fades scars and hyperpigmentation; easily found (whether through ascorbic acid powder to mix into moisturizer or a quick squeeze of lemon juice rinsed off after 5 minutes). Cons: Can tingle and increase skin sensitivity—test on a small patch of skin first and SPF is a must.

VITAMIN E—Pros: Great for stretch marks and burns; wrinkle-releaser—try it around eyes and on forehead; anti-inflammatory; easy—puncture a gel capsule with a safety pin and squeeze. Cons: Better as an overnight treatment than as part of your day routine; it's recommended that you mix it with another oil, like jojoba, or your nightly face cream.

If you can't be bothered with any of these or don't trust our expertise and general brilliance, we recommend memorizing these three words and setting up an auto-delivery on your beauty website of choice: "Weleda Skin Food." It's the only mass-produced (yet all-natural) product we've found that keeps us ash-free and sexy-looking for under a tenner. Plus, it's European and you can tell everyone you got it on your last weekend abroad or some such wealthy nonsense.

TOUCH YOURSELF

We do totally think you should masturbate, but now is the time to improve your life through acupressure.

Press your index finger or thumb into the following areas at around a 90-degree angle. Move your fingers around until you feel a slight tenderness or pulse. Apply pressure until it feels like

> **Spring for a ten-minute back massage at your local cheap nail salon.**

you're getting into some tension, but not so much that you're in a ton of pain.

Speaking of, don't be an idiot. Get professional treatment when you know you need it: This is for minor pain management only. We're not out here tryna get sued.

TW5, OR "THE OUTER GATE": For when you've right swiped too often. Find it by turning your arm palm-side down. You know the two bones that make up your forearm? Use your thumb to measure about a thumb's length down from your wrist and press gently between them.

P6: This is basically the same pressure point as above, except on the underside of your arm. P6 feels especially good when carpal tunnel is ruining your life.

LI10 OR "POOL AT THE BEND": "The bend" equals your elbow. Bend your arm, and measure three fingers' width down from your elbow on the side of your arm facing away from you.

L14: For your headaches (also constipation!). We had a potentially sadistic teacher who taught us this one. Whenever we lowly fifth graders complained of headaches, he wouldn't let us go to the nurse, but instead offered us "the aspirin cure." We'd hold out our weak, still-baby-plump hands, and he'd squeeze the skin between our thumbs and forefingers so hard that even the most badass eleven-year-old delinquents yelped. We hate to admit he had something right—this one feels great as hell when it isn't sprung upon you by Mr. Bernard circa 1999.

And connected . . .

Don't try to pull that "but red wine is good for your skin!" shit. If you feel hungover, you probably look hungover, too. Here's how to look more like a human in ten minutes.

* Drink two big glasses of water to flush out the poison you guzzled.
* Grab whatever (SPF 30 or more!) moisturizer you have on hand. Put it on your face. Lavender oil is also nice, and generally won't break you out, but don't you dare leave the house without sun protection, unless you want to look twice your age by the time you're forty. This is coming from

two people with melanin who care about the world being a more beautiful place, and also all of our friends NOT dying of skin cancer. Do it.

* Using just your middle finger, glide from just below your eyebrows and just below your under-eye circles, moving toward your outer eye.
* Press from just outside your nostril to below the apples of your cheeks. You're always moving outward here, which helps move toxins toward your lymph nodes and helps you depuff.
* Using two or three fingers this time, apply pressure from your temples, down over your jaw muscles, jaw, and all the way to your collarbone.
* Repeat. Avoid a shame spiral. Breathe.

KITCHEN DEEP CONDITION

We don't have enough room here to tell you why shampoo is a scam, but what we WILL say is that deep conditioning is essential for hair of any length. (We both currently have short hair and know of what we speak.) Honestly, the best way we've found to condition our hair is with common cooking oils that you can pick up at Trader Joe's.

* Grapeseed oil (the lightest of the bunch; better for thinner, straighter textures)
* Olive oil (a good neutral; great for breaking or damaged hair)
* Coconut oil (recommended for dull hair, curls, and coils)

If you're using olive or grapeseed oil, add a squeeze of orange, lavender oil, or a few drops of vanilla for scent. Apply as much as you need to coat your hair in a mask. Then twist it up in a towel (best for thick, straight hair) or T-shirt (for curly and thinner hair) that you don't mind getting messy. If your hair is kinky, co-wash and then rinse well; if it's straighter, shampoo once or twice.

DIY Foot Peel

WE KNOW, you expected a face mask recipe here, didn't you?! But no, because basically every book with a beauty DIY section has one of those, and you've probably been putting weird mixes of oatmeal and banana and egg white on your face since you were a fifth grader. Everyone knows sheet masks exist for $4 at this point. So. Enter your DIY FOOT PEEL.

First, google "baby foot peel" to see if you can handle the intensity of what you're about to bless yourself with. For some of you, this will be gross satisfaction enough, and for that you are very welcome.

What you're essentially about to do is create your own acidic chemical peel to encourage cell turnover on your cracked, yellowing heels and toes. The dead, flaky skin will peel off (again, see any number of Highly Detailed message boards), leaving you with fresh, soft feet that you will undoubtedly keep abusing with cute, uncomfortable shoes.

WHAT YOU'LL NEED

Aspirin: the old school, uncoated kind

A lemon

Water

Two clean plastic grocery bags (check for holes)

Thick socks you don't mind messing up

Your roommate's Hulu password so you have two hours
  of sedentary entertainment at the ready

> **Clean your bathtub. Take a bath.**

HOW YOU'LL DO IT

1. Soak your feet in warm water for 20 minutes.

2. Gather the rest of your supplies and sit somewhere comfortable.

3. Crush up 10 to 12 aspirin into a fine powder.

4. Mix the powder with the juice of the lemon—about two tablespoons is a good guide.

5. Add water slowly, a tablespoon at a time, until you have a chalky paste. If you need more aspirin to thicken the mixture, now is the time to add it.

6. Coat your feet in the mixture, focusing on particularly rough areas.

7. Place a plastic bag over each of your feet, then cover them with the socks. Technically, this is so you CAN walk around if you have to, but we suggest taking the next couple of hours as an enforced break from reality. Keep the mixture on for at least an hour, but no longer than two.

(continued)

> **Inexpensive white towels get soft with time. Once they start to yellow, it's time to replace them.**

8. Trash the plastic bags and rinse your feet well.
9. Moisturize with coconut or olive oil . . . or whatever lotion you have on hand (ahem, Weleda Skin Food). Cover your feet in thick socks and feel productive.

Over the next week, you should notice your feet beginning to flake and peel. For some people this will be DRAMATIC, while others might just notice slightly more productive exfoliation in the shower. Either way, we suggest wearing socks and closed-toe shoes for a while, just to not make a mess. And now you can wear sandals without grossing out the general populace!

MICELLES, MY BELLES

If you buy ONE beauty item because of this book, make it micellar water. It used to be one of those "French Pharmacy Buys to Pick Up on Your Next European Vacation" items you saw on listicles back in

> **When considering a major beauty move, remember: You will never be this young or this stupid again.**

2008, but you can definitely get it off-brand at your local CVS now. Hurray for globalization!

Micellar water is a mix of tiny beads of not-quite-oil molecules called surfactants, which are way too science-y and magical to get into here, and soft water, which has lower concentrations of scum-causing minerals like calcium and magnesium. The surfactants attract oil to themselves, leaving your skin moisturized but not slick. Since it's alcohol-free, it won't dry you out like a traditional toner, and you don't have to rinse it off. Great for mornings when you're running out the door but don't want to be a totally trash human: you can swipe it on with a cotton ball, layer with SPF, and feel like you made an effort.

Enter the Underwear Workout

Ideal for when you don't have your gym clothes with you or you're too burdened by the weight of the world/the current news cycle to leave your bedroom but realllly need endorphins. We're not saying the following will make you swole, but it will make you swole-er and happy-ish and less stressed.

WHAT YOU'LL NEED

Underwear. Or not—do you, you look great!

Enough room to lie down for stretching.

Hand weights. But anything can be a hand weight: a filled-up Nalgene, *The Goldfinch* by Donna Tartt, a can of beans . . .

Playlist of music you love. Like, LOVE love. No one is judging you if it's, like . . . Mahler, or the original cast recording of *Oklahoma!,* or Good Charlotte.

HOW YOU'LL DO IT

1. Turn up your music. Do each of the following for the full length of a song (or do only the starred exercises if you're really crunched for time . . .):

2. Stretch it out*

3. Jumping jacks*

4. Biceps curls with hand weights

5. Jumping lunges*

6. Overhead triceps extensions with hand weights

7. Squats

8. Planks—30 seconds, then 20 seconds resting*

9. Stretch it out*

In 16 to 35 minutes, you should be feeling like a human being! If you filled a Nalgene, drink the water (no waste) and call it a day.

CHAPTER 5

HOW TO FASHION

WHEN/WHERE/HOW TO
SEND OUT YOUR LAUNDRY

Ask yourself: Will spending money to take this shortcut (a) give me the time to do something concrete that will benefit me even more financially/emotionally/professionally or (b) keep me from ruining and therefore needing to replace something more valuable? If the answer to either of these is yes, then congratulations, you're allowed to let someone else wash your undies.

We recommend this tip most if you're in an urban area where fluff 'n' folds run something like $1 a pound and many people don't have laundry in their own buildings. If you, like, OWN a washer/dryer, shut the fuck up and thank your deity of choice for the immense privilege they have bestowed upon thyself. As long as you aren't doing all of your towels and all of your sheets every week, $9 should cover your sweaters, shirts, and jeans and is a fairly reasonable sum.

That doesn't mean you're off the hook for checking labels. If you give the laundromat staff a bag full of dry-clean-only stuff and get mad when it comes back a size too small, that's your fault, not theirs. Other items to consider giving a wash in the sink or tub and air-drying: swimsuits; delicates like bras and thin tees; anything with embroidery, fringe, or applique; fleeces; and athletic wear.

> " Every winter, leave $10 in your coat pockets
> before tucking them away. (Maybe this is what
> they mean by "investing"? Or, as our editor,
> Emma, pun-tastically pointed out,
> "in-VEST-ing," lol, we love her.) "

SALVATION ARMY RULES

Things You Should Thrift:

* Anything you plan to wear oversize.
* Basics that are unlikely to cycle trends too quickly: A-line skirts, button-down shirts, straight trousers, sweaters made from natural fibers.
* Costume jewelry.
* Super-super-super trendy pieces. You can try them out used and see how they suit you before you splurge.
* Jeans to cut into jorts.
* Halloween costumes.
* For the curly-and kinky-haired among us, silk scarves for sleeping headwraps.

Things You Should Not Thrift:

* Anything missing a zipper, with a ripped lining, or shoes with worn soles or heels: You'll never actually fix it, and it might be more expensive than buying new, anyway.

* Swimsuits and underwear.

* Beware polyester: It holds smells.

* Shirts with stained armpits: The reason they were donated was that the owners couldn't get them out themselves.

> "
> After you've done that three-week pile of laundry, don't fold and put it away immediately. Go through what's left in your drawers first. What's left are things that aren't part of your usual rotation. You know you never wear them and are keeping them for no very good reason. (Exceptions apply for specialty items like swimsuits/snow gear, outfits for weddings, fancy lingerie, and sports apparel.)
> "

CHAPTER 6

TRAVEL: THE BROKE AND THE RESTLESS

THE OFFICIAL *$9 THERAPY* TRAVEL PACKING LIST, WITH APOLOGIES TO JOAN DIDION

Joan Didion's essay collection *The White Album* includes a packing list that has been riffed on so many times she's basically the James Brown of literature.

Here's our version for a two-to-five-day trip, which, we promise, will save you at least fifteen minutes of stress every time you pull down your carry-on.

In Your Suitcase

* ALWAYS PACK A SWIMSUIT IN CASE A SEXY PERSON APPEARS WHO WANTS TO WHISK YOU AWAY TO ACAPULCO. Also a passport for this reason, even if you're just going to your cousin's place in Boise.
* Two things to cover your lower half (we aren't going to call these "bottoms" because it makes us giggle).
* Two things to cover your upper half: one short-sleeved, one a button-up type that you can layer as a cardigan. Joan is brilliant in that the leotards she suggests DOUBLE AS UNDIES. So do consider the bodysuit route.

Bra

Swimsuit

1 pullover Sweater

Button up top (doubles as cardigan)

2 x Tops

Bodysuit (doubles as undies)

2 x Shoes

Vape

2 x "Bottoms"

Bourbon

Loungewear

> **" Pack a string of fairy lights to turn even the dreariest travel photo into instant spon-con. "**

* One pullover sweater (if going somewhere FANCY, like a wedding, replace with FANCY outfit).
* Two pairs of shoes.
* Socks.
* Bra/underwear. Make sure you like the stuff you pack, again, in case of a sexy stranger but also because life is too short to wear ugly or uncomfortable things near your bits.
* Stretchy top and bottoms to wear on plane and as nightwear.
* CBD vape pen or tincture. Alternately, go with Joan's OG choice of bourbon.
* Bag with travel-sized toothbrush and paste, razor, ibuprofen, tampons/pads/diva cups if you are a menstruating person, micellar water wipes (no spills and can also be used to freshen up if camping or on a very long layover), Emergen-C or Airborne, face cream, SPF. No one cool washes their hair anymore, so skip shampoo.

* If you are a makeup wearer, there's more here depending on your lewk, but keep in mind all you really need is black eyeliner and one lipstick to look like you just had sex (applying with fingers is the trick). Comb or brush; pick one based on texture.

To Carry On

* A giant scarf to use as plane blanket/paparazzi shield.
* Sunglasses for the same reason.
* Prescriptions and deodorant.
* The smallest version of whatever tech you REALLY need. Download a word processor to your iPhone, a reading app, and some ebooks, and your briefly written emails will have an air of busy importantness. This is true even when traveling for work.
* Six-foot-long charging cord with a wall plug.
* Pen.
* One real book or magazine to impress cute seatmates. (Look, we are trying to get you laid on vacation, here.)
* Hand sanitizer. Transportation is filthy.
* House key.
* Wallet.

LETTER OF
RECOMMENDATION:
HOW TO STAYCATION
PROPERLY

There are tons of reasons you might be considering a staycation. Maybe it's too last-minute to pull something else together. Maybe even a bus ticket and modest Airbnb share are financially out of the question. Maybe you have houseplants, or pets, or siblings, or kids, or parents who you'd like to hang out with, too. Maybe you have anxiety or just don't want to deal with other humans.

All of those reasons are super valid, and personally, they've all been reasons we've chosen to stay close to home on our days off.[*]

Here's the perfect plan for a not-lame staycation.

You need:

A REALITY CHECK: First accept that this will never be a vacation. You will not magically emerge as fresh-faced and

---

[*] And if we can digress and be backseat financial advisers for a second . . . if you're lucky enough to have a job that gives you paid vacation days, there's no excuse not to take them. They're part of your compensation, and not using them is actually the equivalent of throwing away money (we were very depressed when we realized this).

stress-free as if you'd spent the week living off the land in Montana or at a yoga retreat in the Catskills, unless your lifestyle is already one of peace and serenity at all times. (In which case, thank you for buying this book, but please stop reading this *immediately* and give it to one of the 44 million Americans with student debt.) The cliché that something is better than nothing 100 percent plays out here. Getting into the spirit of what you love is all still in your grasp.

A DREAM: *What works for you?* What relaxes you? What's your wildest-dreams fantasy of a good time? Identify it, and fake it for cheap.

Here are some sample daylong itineraries to kick you off.

× **LAZY BEACH TRIP:** Don't underestimate the perks of vitamin D: they are real. We're assuming that if you can't make this dream archetype work, you're stuck inland or the weather is shit. But start the day outdoors, if you can. As dog-lovers, here's a rec for a dog-park trip, because animals are magic and if you make friends with one enough to pet it, you get a bonus endorphin boost. Now, listen, this will sound cheesy. But go out and buy a beach towel and your oceanside beverage of choice (S.Pellegrino with an umbrella in it, light beer, white wine in a lemonade bottle so you don't get a $250 fine for drinking in a national park, etc.). Head home, turn on a space heater, lie down, and put on some wave sounds. Nap. Eat a picnic. Get warm and lazy and CHILL. When you're ready to get back to the real world, take a lukewarm shower, give yourself a foot rub with some coconut oil (sunscreen smells!), and watch the sun set.

✷ **EXPEDITION:** The idea of this one is to spark a different mind-set by playing around with your space. In the morning, get active. If you normally swim, go for a run. Cut leg day and flow through a yoga sequence on YouTube. Most fitness studios and gyms will have introductory free trials or first-timer discounts, so mix it up (but remember to cancel before they auto-charge your credit card). When you're home, plan a sightseeing trip of things in your town you've never bothered to check out before. This could be taking a tour of a weird old building, or wandering a neighborhood you're not familiar with, or making a playlist for a long drive and hitting the road. Be sure you're home for an early dinner: pick a brand-new recipe and muddle your way through it. Hopefully you're in time for happy hour at a new bar. Cheers to you for wearing yourself out.

* **SPA:** Go back to our chapter on beauty and do everything we say: face massage, foot peel, deep conditioning, the works. You'll be amazed how tiring it is to be relaxed, so detox with an hour-long hot bath with Epsom salts (which cost about $4 a box). This will basically cure whatever else might possibly be wrong with you. Cook and eat a ridiculously large, healthy meal; something with sprouts and fiber, most likely. Go to bed at 8 p.m.

* **CULTURAL EXCHANGE:** First thing when you wake up, put on a movie with subtitles on repeat. All the sexy foreign actors are your imaginary friends for the day, which is great, because it turns out that people in other countries are just as boring and basic IRL as we are. Go to the library and pick out a book you've been meaning to read for the last six months. Then head to a café and get yourself an espresso (cheap!). Arrange yourself attractively and read ostentatiously until lunch. If there's a museum nearby, go—we're also giving you permission to pay whatever you can afford, so lean into the "suggested" part of "suggested donation" admission. Once again: Arrange yourself attractively and sigh deeply while you have deep thoughts. (This will annoy the other museumgoers, but it's FUN.) While you have dinner, listen to an album all the way through, in

order. No playlists! Curl up with a glass of wine and read until bed, preferably by candlelight.

Avoid these common pitfalls before you start.

* **NOT BREAKING YOUR ROUTINE.** Part of the fun and respite of a vacation is forcing your mind around new paradigms, be they an unfamiliar cityscape, a language you want to practice, or a way of living that's not quite like yours. It's hard to force your mind around another way of living from the same couch where you sit watching Netflix every weekend.

* **NOT IGNORING SOME ASPECTS OF YOUR REAL LIFE.** Ignoring your real life is harder for some people, because it means setting up limits for yourself that might be uncomfortable. It's really okay to take time out to do less. The proof is that *your shit is together enough for you to plan this staycation.* You're not being avoidant, you're putting life on pause the same way you would if you packed a suitcase and jetted off to Bamako.

* **SPACE MIGHT BE TIGHT, BUT IF YOU HAVE A BED, STUFF THINGS UNDER IT.** If you have a closet, fill it up.

Do NOT try to clean everything in your house unless that's your kink. Maybe order in some Seamless instead of slaving over dinner like usual? Take a nap. Drape sheets over half-finished projects. Mute your email alerts and texts for an hour or two each day. You don't have to spend time meditating or journaling or whatnot in order to give yourself permission to zone out.

RELATED: TRAVEL SOLO

One of the biggest realizations of our twenties was that traveling alone is AMAZING. This is how you take a full vacation from your everyday life. What's more relaxing than zero compromises? There's no one to guilt you out of sleeping in if a nap is really what you need or to judge you for ordering three desserts instead of lunch. Nobody's going to try to rush you through taking your own sweet time in a museum or need to be taken care of after one too many drinks with umbrellas in them. And if you're in a place where they speak a language that you don't, there's something super chill about being surrounded by people and yet having space to tune chatter out and live in your own head for a while.

Other Tips for Traveling Like a Glamorous Young Widow:

* Buy a glass of wine on the flight—something we don't fully remember about cabin pressure or altitude gets you drunk faster.
* Wear compression socks with foot cream.
* Pack a set of battery-powered fairy lights to make any location influencer-worthy.
* See uses of pouches; "Hide Your Mess," page 17.
* Whether you're crashing on a friend's couch or roadtripping with family, always pack earplugs.
* Strictly enforce "airplane mode" on your flights and take a goddamn nap.
* Don't be ashamed to face mask—people on the train won't think you look weird, they'll think you're Gwyneth Paltrow.
* Accept that (a) exercise is the best way to beat travel lethargy, but (b) you're not going to ever skip sightseeing to go to the gym. (See "Enter the Underwear Workout," page 97).

The average American man reads one book or less a year. Yet another reason we're considering moving to New Zealand.

Reading is great because you look cute doing it, you can do it for free (we love you, libraries!), and even if it's not always self-improving, it's at least entertaining. Here are some of our and our friends' go-tos if you need inspiration the next time you're in the stacks.

1. Basically any genre fiction—noir, romance, thrillers. The pleasure of genre fiction's sticking to a formula is that you know what you're in for: the hero is going to brood, the girl is going to get the guy (and lots of orgasms along the way), or a burly ex-marine is going to stop the baddies from blowing up the Capitol . . . yet again. A couple of faves to get you started: *Murder on the Orient Express* by Agatha Christie, *Queenpin* by Megan Abbott, *The Cuckoo's Calling* by Robert Galbraith, and anything by Courtney Milan, Alyssa Cole, Cat Sebastian, and Jennifer Crusie.

2. *The Self-Sufficient Life and How to Live It* by John Seymour:

"It's a guide to everything homesteading, from tomato pests to how remove a boulder from your field before you plow it. The illustrations are beautiful and the tone is so matter-of-fact that I can almost see myself in overalls, holding a bushel of my own produce, like Oprah's Instagram." —Miya Kumangai, tarot expert and Justin Peck fan.

3. *Call Me by Your Name* by André Aciman: "I reach for this novel when I'm feeling reflective. It's gutting, but ultimately cathartic." AND *Another Brooklyn* by Jacqueline Woodson: "This novel's aching haze of nostalgia inspires stillness." —novelist John Glynn, author of *Out East* and attender of more weddings than anyone we know.

4. *The Hobbit* by J.R.R. Tolkien: "Not to be confused with the soulless CGI-cash-grab that hit the silver screen. The actual *Hobbit* is a cozy adventure of a bumbling little hero who instantly becomes the reader's spirit animal and is filled with warm joy and cooling wisdom. (Plus delightful descriptions of food and drink.) Reading the first line makes me melt into the couch pillows as if I was going to fall through to Middle Earth below." —Adrian Louis Chandler, writer, story editor, and Disneyland fan.

5. *My Life in France* by Julia Child and Alex Prud'homme: I mean, it's about learning to cook in your gorgeous home(s)

in France, a lifestyle to which we all aspire. The passage about eating her first *loup de mer* will fill you with such intense food lust that it's obscene. Plus, there's the diplomatic service, crazy housemaids, pipes freezing in the Childs' apartment, and her *savage* disdain for Marseille fisherwomen who can't agree on the right recipe for bouillabaisse.

6. Anything by Samantha Irby. Honestly. Anything.

7. *Slow Days, Fast Company* by Eve Babitz: Hands down, the coolest LA girl writing about the coolest LA things. Babitz is the girl who stayed up all night drinking with beautiful people before somehow churning out some of the best personal journalism of the twentieth century.

8. *Pride and Prejudice* by Jane Austen: "I reread it (or parts of it) whenever stuff like dating is stressing me out, because with *P&P* I actually know what's going to happen, and it's all going to work out. And it's just a nice world to be in!"—Annette Berg, who is basically a Danish supermodel.

9. *Real Simple* magazine: "The remarkably soothing power of *Real Simple* magazine is that it transports you to a world where new ways to use a clipboard, finding the right shade of white for your living room, and Ikea furniture–building hacks are headline worthy." —Kate Hutchinson, literary #influencer and biz dev diva.

10. *My Soul Looks Back* by Jessica B. Harris: Conjuring a bohemian New York, a cookbook author and food historian looks back on her friendships with luminaries like James Baldwin, Nina Simone, and Toni Morrison—usually over sumptuously described meals and wine in West Village restaurants.

11. *In the Hand of the Goddess* by Tamora Pierce: "When the world is *wild,* I go to an even *wilder* place: In this middle-grade fantasy classic (yes, I know), a teenaged girl disguised as a boy trains to be a knight, falls in love with a prince, and faces off against an evil mage. Also, she has a psychic connection with her cat. She's my favorite heroine of all time, and my problems are pretty basic compared to hers, honestly." —karaoke goddess Estelle Tang, senior editor at vogue.com.

12. *People I Want to Punch in the Throat* by Jen Mann: "I love listening to comedic, complaining, self-parody, memoir-type audiobooks that parallel aspects of my life, so I can laugh/cry with someone who totally gets me while commuting on the train. And I check them out from the library, so even including train fare, it's way less than $9 total." —Julia Voss, who, trust us, is just smarter than you.

13. *An Unnecessary Woman* by Rabih Alameddine: Aaliya Saleh, a tart seventy-two-year-old Lebanese woman whose solitary life belies a brilliant, literary mind, looks back on her life in this 2014 novel. It's about nothing and everything, but slipping into her seemingly ordinary life is a joy.

14. *Was She Pretty?* by Leanne Shapton: This book will make you feel so fondly toward your exes. Ideal for when you're in the post-breakup/redownload-Tinder phase and need to remember there are nice people out there.

15. *Changing My Mind* by Zadie Smith: You could describe the experience of reading this book as talking for hours with your most brilliantly agile-minded and hilarious friend . . . but honestly, none of our friends are quite as cool as Zadie Smith, so there's no comparison. This is a nonfiction essay collection on everything from *Middlemarch* to 50 Cent's biopic. In a word: perfect.

16. *The New Yorker*: "Am I the only one who first flips to the caption contest when cracking open a new edition? Readers' cleverness makes me feel genuinely hopeful about the collective brain, and it's the one thing I can say I finish in every magazine." AND *Becoming* by Michelle Obama: "It'll make you feel like a third in the Obamas' marriage, which

would be the ultimate act of self-care." And There Is No Shame in True Trash: "Every now and then I google Kristen Stewart and read banal stalker press about my beautiful Bella. Validating a hot celebrity's lack of privacy is the ultimate indulgence." —novelist and cheese afficionado Georgia Clark, author of *The Regulars* and *The Bucket List.*

17. *The Journals of Sylvia Plath*: "Confession: I have never finished this book, and I kind of never want to. I've been nibbling away at it for the past six years or so, ingesting a few pages here and there when I need to disengage from the world and immerse myself in the meandering minutiae of a brilliant mind." —Carla Bruce-Eddings, writer and confirmed Slytherin.

CHAPTER 7

BUILD BOUNDARIES, NOT WALLS

Nick posted a screenshot of this email and got SO many replies from friends asking how this is possibly done. There is no short way to self-help your way out of a lack of boundaries. But with a little discipline, you'll learn to block out the anxieties that can absolutely ruin you if not properly managed. Our own journey toward subverting our anxious/avoidant attachment patterns (google it) has taken years and plenty of professional therapy and natural God-given willingness to be a binch. But since this is a book about living well on the cheap, we'll give you a set of poor man's exercises you can do that may just keep you afloat while you figure out how to pay for professional help.

I AM NOT YOUR ANXIETY'S KEEPER

Once upon a time in book publishing, Nick got assigned to work for this person who stepped on his every nerve. She'd ask him to do all this busy work to keep her organized, despite the fact he had a better eye for books and didn't need someone to keep his work organized for him. And though Nick was going through the motions of appeasing her and grinning through the growing spite, he'd already set his sights on the exit sign. So even while Nick was trying to stay motivated to do his job right, he also cared less and less about the tribulations of being an associate editor.

Now, did Nick also have a case of unmedicated major depression? You betcha. But as his therapist pointed out over and over, even though Nick *knew* he was doing a good job, he was sponging up all of her anxieties and nastiness and then bawling his eyes out in Central Park on his lunch breaks. He was taking all of her anxieties and making them his own. But just a few months into this hellish arrangement, she quit! All her drama and nastiness turned out to have been one million percent about her inability to hack it in her own role. It was like clouds had parted and Nick could finally see how little it had to do with him.

Unfortunately, when he was in the thick of it, keeping boundaries around his work and not letting it ruin his real life wasn't so easy.

One thing that is *very* hard to do is distinguish between being good at a particular job and being Good writ large. That's especially hard because a lot of managers confuse their employees' *motivation* with their employees' *character*. And that type of manager usually loves to talk to you about it. But you, dear reader, won't make that mistake. Motivation is the drive that keeps you coming to the job and getting that day's shit done. Character helps you make good decisions—like the decision, once the day's travails of giving shits are complete, to go home, and return to fight another day. In a healthy situation, there is a boundary between motivation and character.

A manager who confuses the boundary between motivation and character may accuse you of not *caring* enough to do three days' work in one. And this can be triggering if you're ambitious—that's why they said it. If you're this type you're probably someone who wants to give 134 percent to your job, to school, and to your family while keeping your eyes on your next professional leapfrog. But that would mean you're putting in 572 percent in any given week. We know you're magic, but you're not *that* magic. And we know the shame spiral of not being A+ in every facet of your life. To reach any kind of peace, you're going to, at some point, need to prioritize.

You're going to need to put boundaries around some stuff so you can focus on what matters most.

So it's totally fine to use a sick or vacation day every once in a while for what we like to call the Mental Health Day. Unlike a Get Your Shit Together Day, this can be a day when you do absolutely none of what you're supposed to. Or, if what's weighing you down is the mountain of laundry you haven't gotten to because work or family has consumed your life, spend the day at the laundromat with a good book. Now, of course, don't leave your teammates seriously in the lurch if you can avoid it. All their plaintive texts will keep the Mental Health Day from being useful to you anyway, so wrap or pause your projects and then silence your notifications. And truly, managers don't want employees with such poor judgment that they can't see when they're running themselves ragged. If it means you can come back after a day of Netflix and laundry ready to conquer that spreadsheet or phone that horrid client back, everybody will thank you.

CATASTROPHE LIST

The next time you're in bed staring into the dark worried about what catastrophe will befall you next, hop up and do this exercise. It might not get you back to sleep right away, but it will help the rational part of your brain understand that things can get better.

Make a list of possible catastrophes. Each catastrophe on your list will have two entries beside it: (1) The Worst That Could Happen and (2) What You'll Do If It Does. Your list will look something like this:

THE CATASTROPHE	THE WORST THAT COULD HAPPEN	WHAT YOU'LL DO IF IT DOES

Let's say you've enrolled in an introductory corporate finance class after work because you've decided that a career toiling as an associate book editor won't afford you the lifestyle to which you wish to become accustomed. (Just hypothetically.) And there's a test coming up that will end up being a full 25 percent of your grade. Due to the aforementioned evil boss, her unrealistic deadlines, and the general impracticality of working and being in school at the same time, you bomb the test. This could cause mild to severe panic. But never fear! You're going to put things into perspective with your Catastrophe List.

Your first pass at the list might look something like this:

THE CATASTROPHE	THE WORST THAT COULD HAPPEN	WHAT YOU'LL DO IF IT DOES
Bombed your test	*You get a C or D in this class*	*Study extra hard for test 4*

And indeed, that would be a good start. In this example, you've still got time to recover your overall grade by working really hard before the last exam. Even so, you're a little too zoomed in to see the big picture here. Just because you didn't ace every single test doesn't mean all is lost: You still absorbed valuable knowledge and skills from the class. And, since you're taking this class basically for fun, getting a C isn't really the worst-case scenario. Really, your list should look like this:

THE CATASTROPHE	THE WORST THAT COULD HAPPEN	WHAT YOU'LL DO IF IT DOES
C+ or B- in a class taken for fun	*Repeat class if you go to business school after all*	*Fuckin' kill it at corporate finance later*

Okay, so this example is maybe not the most high stakes. But as you might have put together, it's a real example, and the thing about anxiety is that when you're at the cliff's edge, it doesn't matter if it's a mountain or a molehill. And, more important, it's a great way to keep things in perspective when every little thing that goes wrong feels like another boulder you're juggling overhead. Try it for days when you blow your budget or your girlfriend is driving you nuts, too.

CONCLUSION:
WE NEED TO TALK

After dispensing all this advice and spinning yarns that make us seem fabulously chic, you might be thinking we have all our shit figured out, lulz.

While writing this book, we collectively went through about twenty mental breakdowns. Nick and his boyfriend decided to move in together (good), went apartment hunting (bad), and dealt with family illnesses (very bad). Meg attempted to teach her dog to "lie down" (evidently impossible?), saw her company go through a multinational merger with thousands of layoffs (fucking terrifying), and downloaded and deleted her online dating apps six times without ONE SINGLE date 🙄. And then consider that all of those life changes were magnified by the medically induced anxiety and depression we both carry every day. It's bullshit to expect yourself to always be a badass or carefree, so we call foul on basically every other self-help book we've ever read. Sometimes you find the apartment of your dreams; sometimes you unexpectedly have to pay a $1,000 pet fee to your new landlord.

So, please: Do go to therapy.

While we hope this book will help you make your house sparkle and your feet smooth and your parties sing, there are no quick fixes for the unhelpful feelings, self-talk, and behavior patterns that undergird everything humans do. In the modern world, there are more options than ever for finding the support you need to feel mentally healthy. And while friends or family can help you talk it out, we've found combining their cheerleading with the point of view of someone who can be more objective—and, more important, has professional training—essential.

Some people have cultural reasons for thinking therapy isn't for them. In our own communities, we've seen a stiff-upper-lip philosophy keep people from seeking help. But even more troublingly, we've also experienced race- and gender-based biases affecting the kind of mental health care friends and family have been offered.

Luckily, in a world that's much more messed up than any of our brains, there are more ways than ever to get help. Nick started seeing his therapist of seven years at a psychotherapy center where supervised students offered low-cost treatment as they studied for their licenses. Most therapists we know of offer sliding-scale (or even sometimes FREE) counseling based on need. If you're a student, your high school or university probably has a counseling and mental health office. Check your place of worship, gym, or community center. And, tea: if even taking the time to schedule an appointment seems herculean, there are plenty of free and low-cost apps to bring mindfulness strategies and mental health providers to your phone.

Your shit is different from our shit. We don't know what'll work for you, but we hope you'll keep looking.

And in the meantime: unfollow him, go for a walk, take a shower, buy a fern. We think you're super cute and your hair looks great.

Yours in exhaustion and athleisure,
Meg and Nick

ACKNOWLEDGMENTS

NICK:

This book would never have come to pass if co-author, play sibling, neighbor, and dog aunt Megan hadn't one day pranced over to my desk at Simon & Schuster to introduce herself. Thanks for inviting me on the *$9 Therapy* journey—I couldn't have done this without you.

I'd also like to acknowledge our editor, Emma Brodie, in whose eye this project first twinkled. And Wendi Gu, the most effortlessly cool, competent, and collected agent in all of publishing. To everyone at HarperCollins: I know how much time and care you've given this book. And thank you, Janklow & Nesbit, for all your hard work securing the bag!

An immense debt of gratitude to Sabrina Hersi Issa, Aminatou Sow, and Ann Friedman for teaching me about "personal inventory days." In typical Nick fashion I managed to turn a positive into a self-criticism, rechristening them the " 'Get Your Shit Together' Days" in chapter 1. I promise to get around to fixing it on the twenty-fourth of the month.

The deepest of hat-tips to my first real writing mentor, the doyenne of diction, queen of constructive criticism, wearer of pearls and leather, Mary Kay Glazek.

To Ogden James Dolan Greene, my pwoofreader, companion, familiar, and patronus, I know you can't read this but I love you anyway.

To my IRL therapist, Konstantine Pinteris, who has saved my life more than once.

I love you, Ben Yahr; you're perfect.

MEG:

Our editor, Emma Brodie, can turn a boozy summer lunch into a book in a blink. She is the personification of all the things I love most about having publishing friends.

My agent, Wendi Gu, is wise, shrewd, dreamy, enthusiastic, and very fit.

Amy Beager is just the *chicest*. I am so thankful for the talent she lent to these pages.

Thank you to every assistant at Morrow Gift/HarperCollins and Janklow & Nesbit. I wish I could give you all raises.

The Inner Sanctum are Kiele Raymond, Seema Mahanian, Jon Cox, John Glynn, Lisa Erickson, Kristen Lemire, Daniel Burgess, Leslie Davidson-Edwards, Julia Fincher, and Danny Loedel. I don't think it's an exaggeration to say that I could not have survived my twenties in New York without them.

My mom, Michelle Harris, and sisters, Hilary Charles and Amanda Reid, are true masters of grounded and generous self-care, from whom I learned every useful thing in this book. (Also, they may be actual magic.)

Thank you to my therapists. Please don't blame them for anything ridiculous I said. I promise, one day I will follow my own advice.

I wouldn't have written this if not for a seven-pound pup who needs to be kept in the lifestyle to which she has become accustomed. Luna is the most expensive free dog in the world, and the anxious, silly smush of my heart. I'm not quite sure what I'm thanking her for, but there is no greater honor than being her emotional support human.

None of this would have been as much fun without Nick, Sanctum founding member, Capricorn icon, and the Kate Beckinsale to my Chloë Sevigny.

We're already over our word count, but if in the last decade you fed me, prayed for me, gave me advice, took me for drinks, proofread anything from a cover letter to a text, helpfully critiqued an outfit, lent me your home, gave me a job, or helped me navigate a book fair: this is for you.

HarperCollins books may be purchased for educational, business, or
sales promotional use. For information, please email the Special Markets
Department at SPsales@harpercollins.com.

FIRST EDITION

illustrations © Amy Beager

Library of Congress Cataloging-in-Publication Data has been applied for.

ISBN 978-0-06-293633-2   33614081687294

20 21 22 23 24   IM   10 9 8 7 6 5 4 3 2 1